In

How to Pro[tect Your Mind] with the Bullet Proof Metho[d of] Invincible Willpower and Accomplish Your Deepest Desires

By Calvin Kennedy

Table of Contents

Introduction

Willpower is a term that's thrown around lightly by the general population. People say they need more willpower in order to complete their diet, or they need more willpower to get their work done, but it's all in jest. In reality, they do need more willpower to achieve their goals, no matter how small or large they are. But most people don't understand what willpower is.

Willpower is an indomitable strength inside all of us that just needs to be strengthened and tapped into in order to achieve whatever it is we desire. It's a combination of self-esteem, self-confidence, healthy habits, internal influences, and external influences that come together to make this pool of energy we can tap into when we need to.

In this book, you're going to learn about what an invincible willpower is and how to achieve one using the bullet proof method of invincible willpower.

All you need to do is keep reading to discover the secret to success.

Chapter One – Why Aren't You Using It?

Did you fail on your most recent diet? Perhaps you failed to meet a deadline for work because you procrastinated? Maybe you just couldn't bring yourself to get out of bed this morning and drink that smoothie like you promised yourself you would?

All of these things have one thing in common. They require effort, or willpower, in order to get them done. Willpower is defined simply as the effort needed to complete an activity. The activity doesn't necessarily have to be something you don't want to do, but in most cases, it is something you might find disagreeable. For example, your most recent exercise routine might have required you to exercise in the morning, a time when you used to eat an enjoyable breakfast. Exercising might be better for you than that doughnut, but who wants to jog a mile rather than eat a sugary confection?

It's no secret that most of us believe we could improve our lives if we had more willpower. If we had more self-control, then we'd be eating right, exercising properly, avoiding alcohol and drugs, saving our money, not procrastinating, and attaining everything we ever dreamed of. What if I told you that's it's not impossible? Obtaining more willpower is an attainable goal, and with more willpower, you'll achieve more than you ever dreamed.

However, a lack of willpower is not the only thing you need to blame for not reaching goals. There are three necessary steps to achieving your goals. The first one is to establish your motivation for change and set the goal clearly. You'll learn how to do this in Part Three: Setting Yourself Up For Success. The second element is monitoring your behavior toward your goal. You'll learn how to do this in Part Two: Using Habits to Override a Lack of Willpower. The final component is the willpower, which you'll learn about in this part. You might be asking why the book is organized backward from the elements. Well, it's important you understand all the steps before you attempt using the information in this book to change your life.

Whether you have a goal of quitting smoking, exercising more, dieting, spending less time on social media, or studying more, willpower is the critical component of achieving that goal. Some might argue it's the most important, but in reality, they're all imperative to attaining success.

So what is this willpower?

Willpower is the capability to resist a short-term temptation in order to obtain your long-germ goals. There's good reason to exercise willpower. First and foremost, it makes you more successful in everything you set out to accomplish.

Take, for example, a study conducted by Angela Duckworth, PhD and Martin Seligman, PhD, both psychologists at the University of Pennsylvania. The study set out to measure the correlation between self-control and a student's success throughout the year. The first step to this study was to figure out the student's level of self-discipline. To do this, the researchers had the students, parents, and teachers complete questionnaires. In addition to the evaluations, the students were put to the test. They had the option of being given a dollar immediately or waiting a week in order to receive two dollars. The students who waited to receive the two dollars were ranked higher in self-discipline.

These students went on to achieve higher grades, school attendance, and higher standardized test scores. Due to these factors, they were later on admitted to competitive high school programs, such as Advanced Placement courses. Their self-discipline was found to be more important than their IQ levels when it came to predicting their academic success (Duckworth & Seligman, 2005).

However, the benefits of willpower extend well beyond students' school years. Terrie Moffitt,

PhD, and her colleagues studied a group of one thousand people from the moment they were born to the age of thirty-two as a long-term health study focusing on self-control. This study found individuals with high self-control as children would grow into adults who had a greater mental and physical health, were less likely to participate in criminal activities, abused less drugs, and had better financial security (Moffitt, et al., 2011).

There are numerous names for willpower: drive, determination, self-discipline, resolve, and self-control. However, a psychology would define willpower in a few different ways.

- The capability to delay gratification, or resisting a short-term temptation in order to obtain a long-term goal.
- The ability to override an unwanted feeling, thought, or impulse.
- The capability to use the cognitive system of behavior rather than the emotional system.

- Effortful, conscious regulations of yourself by you.
- A limited resource that can be depleted.

Logically, it seems like we ought to be using willpower to attain everything we desire, yet a majority of people appear to lack the ability to exercise willpower despite its obvious benefits. There are several reasons for this.

The main reason most people lack willpower is due to their upbringing. Ultimately, the people who teach you how to exercise willpower are your guardians, and if they lack willpower, so will you. If you had willpower when you were a child and young adult, and yet you seem to be lacking it now, then it might be you haven't been exercising it enough lately. Willpower is like a muscle, and when it's not exercised, it will atrophy. The final reason you might not be exercising as much willpower lately is due to chronic stress.

Take note genetics and outside influences were not mentioned in that list. Your genetics have nothing to do with the amount of willpower you're born with, but your upbringing has something to do with the amount you buildup over time. Outside influences may appear to make you feel more stressed; however, you are the one who decides if those outside influences are going to take hold or if you'll let them go.

There is one more fact you should know about willpower; it is not infinite. Every day, you exercise willpower through each decision you make, and your finite source of willpower depletes with each decision. This willpower depletion will be further explored in the following chapter.

Chapter Two – The Willpower Depletion Theory Debunked

It seems that when you need it the most, willpower seems to fail you. Scientists have told their followers that willpower is a finite resource for years, but there are new studies coming out that may be disproving this belief.

When posed with the question of whether or not willpower is finite or infinite, scientists will answer differently from one another, leaving the rest of us a bit confused as to whether or not willpower truly is finite. Some scientists will argue that willpower wears out and is like a muscle. It's exhausted by overuse. Other scientists will argue that your willpower only falters because you believe it's fallible. If you believe you have unlimited self-control, then you do.

There is evidence on either side of the argument. Early studies have supported the theory that willpower is finite, which means that as you make decisions throughout the day, your willpower depletes. One of the earliest studies suggesting willpower is finite demonstrated that it was harder for people to persevere in a mentally challenging task after they had to resist eating something delicious, such as cookies or chocolates. Since then, there have been more than a hundred experiments that reached similar conclusions.

However, there has been more recent research that's challenging the idea that willpower is finite. Several studies have shown a reduced willpower is only seen in those who believe their self-control or willpower is finite. Those who think self-discipline is a function that is maintained over time do not experience the same willpower depletion. In addition, studies demonstrated if you teach people they have an unlimited self-control, then they do. In contrast, if they are taught willpower is finite, then the opposite effect happens.

However, there's new research that suggests both perspectives are correct. In experiments that involved over three hundred undergraduates, researchers demonstrated that believing in unlimited willpower helped shore up a person's resolve when the depletion was mild, but not if a person was already running on fumes (Vohs, Baumeister, & Schmeichel, 2012). When people were seriously depleted, belief in unlimited willpower made things worse.

Baumeister and his colleagues compared students who were supplied with information that suggested their willpower was either finite or infinite. The students were asked to perform tasks that were designed to deplete their self-control. One group was asked to do two such tasks while another had to do double that, and a third group did no depleting tasks.

Those who were in the group asked to do two tasks were assigned to view products and choose between those products. Later on, they were asked to look at words on a computer and respond with the first letter of the color of the word's font. The word was, of course, spelling out a different color than the font it was in. Those who were asked to do the four tasks were asked to watch Eddie Murphy videos while they suppressed their laughter, and then they were asked to read through a document and cross out the letter 'e,' a task that was made more difficult later on when they were asked to only cross out e's where a vowel occurred right after or two letters before the 'e.'

After these challenges, the researchers assessed the student's self-control with two measures, including on where they measured the volunteer's preference for a small immediate reward or a larger one that was delayed. Amongst those who'd completed two tasks, their beliefs about willpower predicted their performance on the self-control tests. Those who'd been primed to believe willpower was infinite did better, but the ones who had to perform four tasks performed worse. Those who believed willpower was finite did just as well or better on the self-control tests.

The final results? It's physical fatigue that affected the students the most. When the students were just beginning to get tired, believing in an unlimited resource helped them perform better, but as they became more fatigued, believing in that unlimited resource turned on them and made them perform worse.

The overall conclusion was, willpower is better used like you're running a marathon. Pacing yourself is imperative because, if you expend all your willpower at once, then positive thinking will not be enough to get you through the day.

Yet, there is another new research paper that suggests the depletion of willpower is much more complicated than just an allocation of resources. Michael Inzlicht, one of the lead authors on the paper, believes that depletion is actually a shift in attention and motivation (Inzlicht & Schmeichel, 2012).

As an example, if you've exercised self-control recently, you might feel you deserve to have a reward. Michael believes that if you work really hard, you feel you deserve a reward, so you just don't feel like exercising willpower anymore. It's not a matter of whether or not you have it, but whether or not you feel like using it.

This motivational balance is able to be manipulated by many different things, such as the belief that willpower is infinite. In Baumeister's notes on his study, he made a notation that students who were encouraged to see the study as being an significant role showed less of a depletion in willpower.

When you're depleted, it's not that you're not able to do something, but it's that you just don't feel like using your self-control. If someone were to put a gun to your head, no matter how fatigued you were, you'd try to do what they said. Therefore, this shifts the question to why you don't want to do something. If you're offered a strong enough incentive, then you're able to overcome not wanting to do something.

Michael also believes attention plays an imperative role in willpower. Those who stop attending to cues that tell them control is appropriate in a situation begin to pay more attention to the fact there's something rewarding. This means that in order to improve your willpower you have to keep many different factors balanced. When you're facing a short-term challenge, believing your willpower is infinite; will help you. For a more stressful, long-term challenge, knowing your limits will help you pace yourself and let you avoid temptations when you're most vulnerable to them. Therefore, being mindful of your attention span, and recognizing when it's break time, can help you.

Studies have found those who have the most self-control don't spend their time resisting temptation, but rather make environments that limit their exposure to temptation. Therefore, you have to battle your internal and external willpower depletion demons in order to obtain infinite willpower, or close to it. So let's look at that in the following chapter.

Chapter Three – Internal Willpower Killers

Internal willpower killers are the more difficult ones to overcome because they come from within, which means you have to change your behavior and beliefs in order to squash them. The top three internal willpower killers are a lack of self-control or discipline, limiting beliefs, and stress caused by anxiety and depression. This chapter will include an explanation of each of these and how they affect your willpower, as well as actions you can take in order to turn your life around.

Lack of Self-Control

The obvious solution to this problem is to avoid temptation altogether. The out of sight out of mind principle works well in this situation. Let's look at a study as an example.

Walter Mischel took preschool children and marshmallows and gave them two choices. They could eat the marshmallow in front of them immediately, or they could sit and wait for two marshmallows for an unspecified amount of time (Mischel, 1989). The children who looked away or closed their eyes were more likely to wait for the two marshmallows, but the ones who stared at the first marshmallow were more likely to take the marshmallow rather than wait for the second one. Therefore, out of sight, out of mind really does work and it can work for adults too. If you're trying to lose weight or you want to stop procrastinating by watching videos on YouTube, then keep candy in your desk drawer rather than on the desk and stop pulling up YouTube when you login to your computer.

Another great way to improve your self-control is a technique known as the implementation intention. These intentions will take the form of an if-then statement that will help you plan for a situation that will likely foil your resolve. As an example, someone who wants to drink less and is attending a party might tell themselves, "If someone asks me what I want to drink, then I'll ask them for a Diet Coke." Research amongst adults has discovered that implementation intentions improve your self-control, even amongst those who've experienced willpower depletion. Having a plan before you head into a situation where you might be tempted can help you make the right decision in the moment without having to draw on your willpower as much.

There's a lot of research out there that suggests people have a finite reservoir of self-control, which suggests that we're destined to fail when we're faced with too many temptations; however, researchers don't believe someone's willpower is ever completely exhausted. Instead, people seem to hold some willpower in reserve that they're conserving for future demands that are more important. The proper motivation lets you tap into those reserves, letting you persevere when your self-control has been depleted.

To demonstrate this theory, Mark Muraven discovered willpower-depleted people persisted on self-control tasks when they were informed they'd be compensated or their efforts would benefit someone else, such as finding a cure for cancer. High motivation could help overcome a weakened willpower to an extent.

In addition, willpower might be made less vulnerable to depletion in the first place. Researchers who are studying self-control describe it as being like a muscle that will get fatigued when it's used heavily. However, there's another aspect to this analogy. While a muscle is exhausted in the short-term, it strengthens over time in the long-term when it's regularly exercised. Therefore, regularly exerting self-control could improve your willpower. Let's look at a study as an example.

Mark Muraven and his colleagues asked some volunteers to follow a two-week plan to track what they ate, improve their mood, or mend their posture. Compared to the control group, the group that exercised self-control by performing their assigned tasks was less vulnerable to their willpower depleting in the follow-up tests (Muraven, 1999). In another study conducted by Muraven, he discovered smokers who practiced self-control for two weeks by squeezing a handgrip and avoiding sweets regularly were more successful at quitting smoking than those who performed two weeks of regular tasks that required little to no self-control, like writing in a diary (Muraven, Practicing self-control lowers the risk of smoking lapse, 2010). Therefore, if you practice self-control on a daily basis with small tasks, such as sticking with not eating sugary snacks or making sure to take your vitamins every day, you'll be more likely to exercise self-control in the future with much more important tasks, such as quitting smoking or achieving your dreams.

Another interesting find is that willpower depletion and a lack of self-control are tied closely with glucose levels in the body. Eating regularly in order to maintain balanced blood glucose levels in the brain can help refuel your willpower resources. However, don't mistake consuming glucose for consuming more sugar in the form of sugary snacks and drinks. Eating a healthy, balanced diet will help you maintain your glucose levels rather than having them crash.

In addition, evidence from willpower-depletion studies suggests creating a list of goals to be completed and looking too far into the future can deplete willpower. Being depleted in one area will reduce the willpower in other areas, so it makes sense to focus on a single goal at a time. So in other words, it's not a good idea to try to exercise self-control by trying to quit smoking, eating healthier, and starting a new exercise regime at the same time. Creating goals and sticking with just one at a time allows you to create healthy habits, which will help you stay on track without depleting your willpower resources.

So in short, you need to:

- Exercise self-control on a daily basis with small tasks, such as doing ten jumping jacks in the morning or drinking a glass of water when you first wake up. This will help build your self-control muscles.
- Avoid putting yourself in situations where there are unnecessary temptations, such as walking outside when all the other smokers are on a smoke break and you're trying to quit.
- Use the implementation intention technique by creating if/then statements for yourself before you walk into a situation where you need to exercise self-control. For example, "If someone asks me if I want dessert, then I'll ask them for a glass of water."

Limiting Beliefs

A limiting belief is a belief that constrains you in some way. By believing in a limiting belief, you do not think, say, or act in a way that would go against this belief, and this limits your life. You might have beliefs about duties, abilities, rights, permissions, and so on and so forth, but limiting beliefs are often about yourself and your self-identity. The beliefs could be about others or the world in general, too. No matter what, they limit you in some way and prevent you from being your best.

Common Limiting Belief Statements
I Can't

People often have a limited self-image of what they are able and not able to do. If someone thinks they cannot dance, then they will never try or never go to a dance lesson to improve their dancing skills. This is the problem with the 'I Can't' statements; you believe your abilities are fixed and you're not able to learn.

I Do/Don't

You might define yourself by what you do or don't do. You might say something along the lines of, "I'm a cashier," which means you don't do accounting and shouldn't ever think about it, and consequently, you fail to sell your services well. Another common one focuses on how you judge yourself. You think, "I don't deserve..." and so you don't expect or find things because of this belief.

I Must/Must Not

People are bound by norms, values, laws, and other beliefs that govern what they must and must not do. Yet, not all of them are mandatory and some of them are limiting. If you think, "I have to clean my room every day," then this robs you of the time you might spend doing something more productive.

Others Are/ Others Will

Just as you have limiting beliefs about yourself, you also have limiting beliefs about others, which can limit you in many ways. If you think of others as being more capable and superior, then you will not challenge them. If you see them as selfish, then you won't ask them for help.

People often guess what others are thinking based on their beliefs about that person. These guesses are wrong, in most cases. Therefore, you might believe they don't like you when they actually don't have an opinion about you, or they think you're a nice person. From your guesses at a person's thoughts, you deduce their likely course of action, which can be completely wrong. Even faced with this evidence, it's surprising how many people hold onto their original beliefs about someone.

I Am/Am Not

Every time you think 'I am,' you're also thinking 'I am not' or 'I can't.' As an example, you might think, "I'm an artist," and so you conclude that you're never going to be good at math or you can't soil your hands with any type of manual labor.

'I am' thinking puts you in the mindset that you can't change. Whether you think 'I'm intelligent' or 'I'm not intelligent,' either belief can stop you from learning. 'I am' leads to generalization, such as 'I'm smart' means 'all of me is all of smart and all of smart is all of me.'

How the World Works

Beyond the limiting beliefs I just mentioned, there are all kinds of other beliefs about how the world works or how the world is, from the property of materials to the laws of nature. This leads to anything from beliefs that all dogs bite to the idea that airplane travel is dangerous.

Causes of Limiting Beliefs

Limiting beliefs come from somewhere, and they're not always from our parents.

Experience

One of the main ways we come across our limiting beliefs is through the experiences we have in life. We act, something happens, and we draw a conclusion about that event. Often, these beliefs can be helpful in our survival, but they can be limiting.

When children are young and do not have a lot of experiences to draw from, they can draw false or limiting conclusions about events, things, or people. Nature created us this way to keep us out of harm's way. Children learn and build their beliefs faster from a harmful experience rather than a good one. For example, a child puts their finger on a hot stovetop and it's painful, so they believe all stovetops are unsafe and they should never touch the stove again. If punching another child results in a beating, then the child might believe they are weak from there on out.

Education

When people are creating their perceptions of the world, they cannot depend on their experiences for everything. They will read and listen to their elders – parents, teachers, guardians – about how the world works and how they need to behave in it.

However, a child's elders are not always the best informed. Children also learn from their peers and are influenced by their beliefs, which might be limiting.

Education can be a double-edge sword because it tells you what's right and wrong and good and bad. It helps you grow and survive, but just because you were taught something, you might never try things and miss out on pleasant and useful knowledge and experiences.

Faulty Logic

When you're making a decision, you make a 'return on investment' estimate and easily conclude the investment of your effort, time, and money is not sufficient, and there is a low chance of success and a high chance of failure. The return might be negative if you're harmed in some way.

People tend to make decision errors, such as making a decision based on a poor estimation of the outcome. They take a little bit of data and generalize it to all of their decisions. They go on hunches based more on subconscious hopes and fears rather than reality.

The word 'because' is a hazardous word. When it's used, it seems like it's being used for a good reason, but this is not always the case. People like to understand cause and effect, and they will often not challenge reasoning that uses rational argument.

Excuses

One reason people use faulty logic and create limiting beliefs is to excuse themselves from what they perceive to be a failure of theirs.

When you do something and it doesn't work, you might explain away your failure by creating and using a belief that justifies your actions and leaves you blameless. However, in doing this, you don't learn and might increasingly paint yourself into a corner, limiting what you think and do in the future.

Fears

Oftentimes, your limiting beliefs are driven by fear. Locking the belief into place is the fear that if you go against this belief, then your deep needs will not be tended to.

There's often a strong social component to the decisions and the thought of criticism, rejection, or ridicule by others is enough to inhibit you. You may fear you might be harmed in some way by someone else, and so you avoid them or you seek to appease them.

A frame of reference is a complex diagram of unquestioned values, beliefs, and so forth that you use when you're inferring meaning. If any part of that frame is challenged or changed, then the meaning that's inferred changes.

If you want to reframe your beliefs, then step back from what's being said and done and consider the diagram or the lens that reality is being created. Understand everyone's unspoken assumptions, including their beliefs and frames of references being used.

Then consider the alternative reality, effectively looking at it in another way. Challenge your beliefs or other aspects of the frame; stand in another one and describe what you see; change the attributes of the frame to reserve the meaning. Ignore or select aspects of words, the frame, and actions to emphasize and downplay certain elements.

Some examples of reframing might be to see a problem as an opportunity for learning, seeing a weakness as a strength, or an impossibility as something that's just a difficult possibility. For example, you're having a hard time paying your bills because you budgeted wrong this month. Rather than seeing this as a negative problem, you can twist it into a positive by making the decision to learn how to become better at saving.

Oftentimes, you can change someone's frame just by changing their emotional state, making them happier, aggressive, and sad, etc. When they're happier, they'll be more optimistic and positive, and so on and so forth.

For an example, someone might say a project cannot get done on time, and you respond with, "What if we were to get some outside help?" By adding a solution, you've changed someone's frame.

Another example might be your friend says something is stupid, and you respond with, "It might appear to be stupid, but it's stupid to not look at the problem again and see what else is able to be done."

Once you recognize a limiting belief in yourself, you can overcome it by educating yourself, changing your mindset, and ultimately changing your belief. However, recognizing those limiting beliefs can be difficult. If something makes you feel afraid, your thoughts start with 'I am', 'I am not', 'I can', or 'I can't'. If you are using logic and beliefs instilled in you from your elders, then you might want to question them. You may be using a limiting belief as an excuse to not make yourself a better person.

A limiting belief about willpower might be, "Invincible willpower is impossible." Challenge that belief by following the steps in this book, and you'll learn that invincible willpower is a very achievable outcome.

Depression, Anxiety, and Stress

The biology of willpower and stress are just not compatible, so anytime you're feeling stressed out, it's difficult to find the willpower to do the things we know we need to do. The fight-or-flight response floods our bodies with energy to act instinctively and takes away from the area of the brain that's necessary for making good decisions.

Stress encourages you to focus on the immediate, short-term goals and the outcomes, but self-control requires that you keep the big picture in mind. Learning how to manage your stress better or just remembering to take a few deep breaths when you're feeling tempted, is one of the steps you can use to improve your willpower.

Sleep deprivation is one of the main causes of chronic stress because it impairs your body's ability to use energy, including your brain. The prefrontal cortex is hit hard by sleep deprivation because it loses control over the areas of the brain that make cravings and govern our stress response. When it's left unchecked, the brain will overreact to ordinary, everyday temptations and stress. Studies have shown the effect of sleep deprivation on your brain is like being drunk.

The good news is any step toward quality sleep can be a great boost to your self-control. Some steps you can take include creating a bedtime routine by going to bed at the same time every night, turning off electronics, and even taking some melatonin twenty minutes before you want to go to sleep. You should not use the melatonin for more than a week because you don't want to develop an addiction to sleeping aids, but it will help you get your circadian rhythm back in order.

Common Ways to Battle Chronic Stress, Depression, and Anxiety

Exercise

Exercise is an excellent way to begin battling stress, and it's a healthy habit everyone should indulge in. Exercise will help distract you from stressful events, and it can lessen the harmful effects of chronic stress on your blood pressure. However, you shouldn't be doing the same exercises day in and day out. You need to vary your exercise program by combing aerobic exercises with strength training exercises. Start out slowly because strenuous exercise for those who are not used to it can be harmful. Here are a few suggestions on how to begin exercising.

1. Take an aerobics class at a gym.
2. Walk briskly for ten minutes a day at lunch time or in the morning after you've woken up. You can also perform this after a stressful event to help burn up the cortisol in your bloodstream.

3. Take a swimming class. This is an ideal exercise for those who are under chronic stress from health complications, such as asthma, muscular diseases, and mental health complications.

4. Try some yoga or tai chi classes. These exercises incorporate deep breathing exercises, which is an added benefit to relieving stress.

Making a plan and executing it in full will provide you with the feeling of control, which is beneficial if you're someone who has limiting beliefs and is stressed all the time. Just ten minutes of exercise three times a week will help build a good base for beginners. Gradually build up the lengths of the sessions to thirty minutes or more, and then add on days when you exercise.

Relaxation Methods

Stress is never going to go away. There will be stressors in your life at all times, but it's how you handle them that determine whether or not they affect you for the long-term. Everyone should develop methods to promoting a relaxation response, or a natural unwinding of their stress response. Relaxation will lower your blood pressure, pulse rate, and respiration, and it'll release your muscle tension, as well as ease your emotional stress. This response is individualized, meaning certain approaches will work for some people and not others. Meditation during the moments before a stressful event can help reduce the stress response without impairing your alertness, memory, or concentration.

Combination of the techniques that will be mentioned will probably work better than just using one at a time. No one should expect the approaches to completely relieve stress, but if they're done on a regular basis, these programs can be effective. Let's look at some examples of relaxation techniques you can start using today.

Acupuncture

There is some evidence that suggests acupuncture is able to improve some of the physical aspects associated with stress and health complications. As an example, acupuncture might improve stress-related heart complications such as heart failure, which might provide a great benefit to patients. However, acupuncture does not have any effect on stress-related heart rates or blood pressure.

Hypnosis

This might benefit some people who are under severe stress. In one study, patients who had irritable bowel syndrome underwent hypnosis and experienced improvements in their bowel movements and bowel symptoms.

Deep Breathing Exercises

When you're stressed out, your breathing naturally becomes more rapid and shallow. Taking a deep breath with automatically make you feel more relaxed and help you wind down. Exercises that incorporate deep breathing will intensify this natural physical reaction and can be useful when you're in a stressful situation, or if you want to maintain a relaxed state throughout the day.

To perform deep breathing at any time, follow these steps.

1. Make sure you're breathing through your nose only and inhale slowly and deeply for ten seconds.
2. Be sure your stomach and your abdomen are expanding and not your chest.
3. Exhale through your nose slowly and deeply for ten seconds.
4. To help quiet any racing thoughts, concentrate entirely on your breaths and counting to ten.
5. Repeat this for five to ten times, and be sure to make a habit of doing this exercise a few times a day, even when you're not feeling stressed out.

Muscle Relaxation

The muscle relaxation technique is often combined with the aforementioned deep breathing technique for the best results. It's easy to learn and useful for helping those who have trouble sleeping because of chronic stress and racing thoughts. In the beginning, it's a good idea to have a friend or a partner check for any tension in your limbs by lifting your arm and dropping it. The arm should fall easily without any tension from you. Practice will make the exercise more effective and produce the relaxation response quicker.

To perform this exercise, follow these steps.

1. After you lie down in a comfortable position with your limbs uncrossed, concentrate on every part of your body.

2. Practice deep breathing throughout the exercise.

3. Tense each muscle one at a time as tight as you can for a count of ten seconds, and then release it. Your muscle should feel completely relaxed and heavy. Start with

the top of your head and keep going down until you get to your feet, where you will curl the toes and then relax them.

4. Once you've gone through your body, imagine tensing and releasing your internal organs.

Meditation

Meditation has been used for years in Eastern cultures, but it's now a widely accepted relaxation technique across the globe. The goal of meditation is to quiet your mind. There have been studies that show regular meditation is able to benefit the heart by reducing blood pressure. You should not meditate for longer than twenty minutes in the morning after you wake up, and then again in the evening before you eat dinner.

Let's look at mindfulness meditation first as it's the easiest to learn.

1. Sit in a chair with your spine straight and comfortable. You can cross your legs or keep your feet firmly on the floor.

2. Close your eyes gently and observe your breath by practicing deep breathing.

3. As your mind wanders, just note that you've wandered and return on the exhale. It might be helpful to imagine your thoughts as clouds floating away or leaves floating down a river away from you.

Another popular technique is known as transcendental meditation. It uses a mantra, such as a word or a chant that has no meaning, to keep you focused. It's practiced the same way as mindfulness meditation but with focusing on the mantra instead of your breaths.

Biofeedback

This technique measures bodily functions, such as your breathing, blood pressure, heart rate, skin temperature, and your muscle tension. By being aware of these movements, you can learn how to alter normally autonomic functions by relaxing or visualizing. This method involves seeing a doctor because you have to be hooked up to a machine in order to know when you've reached a truly relaxed state. When you see a psychologist or a therapist, they will tape electrodes up to your temples and encourage you to relax using the aforementioned methods. Your brainwaves will be measured and there will be an audible sound when you reach the frequency that is associated with deep relaxation. By repeating this process, you'll associate the sound with the relaxed state and learn how to achieve relaxation on your own.

Massage Therapy

This method might decrease your cortisol levels, and some research has shown there's a possible role of physical touch in managing your stress. Many massage techniques are available, such as Swedish, Shiatsu, and Reflexology. It's best that you speak with a massage therapist to determine what type of massage might work the best for you.

Natural Remedies

While there are many claims that natural remedies are able to relax you and relieve chronic stress, there is no such proof that these remedies actually work. However, if you want to try them, then the safest one to begin with is aromatherapy.

Aromatherapy involves putting essential oils into a diffuser or on a cotton swab and smelling them for a short period of time. Some of the most popular essential oils for this purpose are valerian, lavender, and ylang-ylang.

If you decide you want to ingest natural remedies for stress relief, remember they are no different than taking any other medication. You may learn to rely on them more than you should, and you might find yourself experiencing adverse side-effects. Always check with a doctor before you begin a natural remedy regime, especially if you're already taking other medications.

Internal willpower killers are some of the most difficult ones to overcome, but external willpower killers can easily sneak up on you and keep you from achieving your goals. We'll discuss how to destroy them in the following chapter.

Chapter Four – External Willpower Killers

Just as there are external influences for everything else in your life, there are external influences on willpower. Some of these external influences might be healthy, such as a friend that encourages you to go after your dreams and goals, and others may be unhealthy, such as a friend who does the opposite. While you may think you don't have control over external willpower influences, you do. You're able to change your situation, no matter what it is, in order to make your life happier and healthier, so let's get started with some of the influencers of willpower.

Poverty and an Overabundance of Decisions

According to the United States Census Bureau, 13.5% of Americans are below the poverty line. That might not seem like a big number, but that's roughly 43,878,479 Americans who are currently suffering from poverty.

We all struggle with the decisions of whether or not we should purchase an item, such as a new pair of pants, new shoes, a new car, or even a new home. The temptation to purchase something is a very familiar test of will for every adult out there. Just like unhealthy food choices have skyrocketed, so have the opportunities for impulse buys. Banks with ATMs are all over the place, we now have plastic cards that harbor our entire bank account's balance on them, and credit cards if we happen to outspend what we currently have. Online shopping means you can burn through everything without having to leave your own home. And just like other areas of your life, from resisting having too many drinks to overeating, people's purchasing behavior is subject to willpower depletion.

One interesting study on this theory is one conducted by Kathleen Vohs and Ronald Faber. In their study, participants were shown a silent film where a series of one-syllable, common words flashed across the bottom of the screen. Half the participants were instructed to actively ignore the words, which required self-control. The other half were told nothing and were just shown the film. The two groups were then asked to look through product listings for items such as cars and watches, and then they were to report how much they'd spend on each item. Those who had to exert self-control in the video task were willing to spend an average of $30,037 on the items, while those who did not have to exert self-control were willing to spend an average of $22,789 (Vohs & Faber, 2003). Therefore, the participants who had to exercise self-control could not exercise as much self-control on the second task.

In another experiment, Faber and Vohs tested participant's spending behavior by presenting them with the opportunity to buy low-cost products such as playing cards and mugs. Those who'd previously exerted self-control in the lab exercise reported a higher temptation to purchase something. In fact, they purchased a larger number of products and spent more money than the participants who had not performed the willpower depletion task.

It doesn't matter if you're below the poverty line or not; it's more difficult for people to make financial decisions if they've had to make an abundance of decisions throughout the day. However, financial decision-making could be even more challenging for those who are living below the poverty line. Dean Spears, a Princeton doctoral candidate, conducted experiments in India to explore the link between poverty and a person's willpower strength. In one of these studies, he visited two villages. One was wealthier and one was less so, and he offered the people there the opportunity to purchase a popular brand of body soap at a low price. The soap was an excellent deal, but it still represented a difficult financial decision for those who were living in poverty.

Before and after he offered the soap, the participants in the study were asked to squeeze a handgrip, which is a test of self-control strength. Dean Spears discovered the wealthier participants squeezed the handgrip the same length of time before and after their purchasing opportunity. The poor participants squeezed for a much shorter duration after they had to make their decision. Their willpower strength had been lessened by the financial decision-making.

However, there is a silver-lining to all of this. If those who are in poverty are more likely to experience willpower depletion, then reducing the number of hard decisions they have to make throughout the day might help them maintain their stores of self-control for difficult future decisions. Nava Ashraf and her colleagues showed that effect amongst bank customers in the Philippines in their study. They offered customers a chance open an individual savings account with a twist. The customers were only able to withdraw from the account after they'd reached a target amount or date that was set by them. After a year, the ones who were enrolled in the account saved 82% more than those who were enrolled in normal savings accounts (Ashraf, Karlan, & Yin, 2004). Eliminating their decision to spend or save helped the test participants avoid depletion in willpower.

Together, these findings have suggested that those at the low end of the economic spectrum could be particularly vulnerable to breaking down when it comes to willpower. It's not that those who are underprivileged have a lesser amount of willpower than those who are wealthy, but that every decision those who are living in poverty have to make, even if it's just to purchase soap, requires self-control, which dips into their pool of willpower.

So how can you combat this, whether you're someone who suffers from willpower depletion due to financial instability or someone who suffers from willpower depletion due to an overabundance of decisions?

Willpower Depletion Due to Financial Instability Solutions

1. Automate as much as you can. If you have the funds to automate bill payments coming out and deposits being made into your savings accounts, then you'll be making a lot fewer financial decisions on a daily basis.

2. Put money into savings accounts where you can't withdraw as often, such as ones that allow you to withdraw only once a month. You'll save more money in the long run, and you'll save more willpower too.

3. Make shopping into a routine. Instead of going to the grocery store every night, pick one night out of the week when you go, as well as make a budget for how much you're going to spend. Making a financial decision into a routine allows you to step back and know what's going to happen rather than having to make a decision every time.

Willpower Depletion Due to an Overabundance of Decisions Solutions

1. Make routines rather than winging your day. When you have a routine to follow and you know what's coming next, you won't have to make a decision. You'll just go about your day in one fluid motion. That way, when something does come up where you need to make a decision, you have the willpower to choose wisely.

2. Create healthy habits. Habits are what make up routines, such as brushing your teeth before you go to bed. You don't have to make a conscious decision to brush your teeth every night before you go to bed because you've made it into a habit. The following chapter will discuss habits in more detail.

Social Influences

It's no secret that those you surround yourself with are going to influence your decisions. Your decisions are essentially shaped by your closest friends and family when they're around. Breakthroughs in the study of social groups, or network science, have demonstrated how many things people tend to think of being individual, such as whether you quit smoking or eat healthy, are actually collective decisions.

In one study conducted by Nick Christakis of Harvard Medical School and James Fowler of the University of California, San Diego, people's behaviors are contagious. If a friend becomes obese, then you have a 57% higher chance of becoming obese, too (Christakis & James, 2007). A loss of willpower is contagious.

Do this exercise. Think of five people in your life who you spend the most time with. Now rate them on a scale of one to five, one being no willpower and five being infinite willpower. Where do those five people fall? Add that number up, divide it by five, and that's most likely where your willpower is. Other people's willpower influences you.

If you have major goals in your life and you'd like to reboot your willpower, then you should think about the people you're spending time with. Think of the people you know who are the mentally strongest. How can you spend more time with them and be inspired by them? Who triggers you to lose your willpower, and how can you spend a little less time with them? Are you able to ask for help, and if so, who do you know who can keep you accountable?

If you know someone who has absolutely no willpower and they're a completely negative influence on you, then you should think about breaking off your friendship or relationship with them. It might sound harsh, but in order to have infinite willpower, you need to hoard yours and not allow others to suck it out of you.

In the following chapter, we're going to take a look at how you can automate decisions with habits in order to conserve your well of willpower. That way, when you're put in a situation where you have to make a tough decision, you'll have the willpower to make the right decision.

Chapter Five – Creating Invincible Willpower

By this point, you should understand what willpower is and what influences it on a personal level. As an example, some people might suffer from a depletion of willpower because they have to make hard decisions every day due to financial difficulties, while others might lack willpower because their self-esteem is not up to par. This chapter is going to walk you through the personal steps you need to take in order to address your willpower killers and develop an invincible willpower.

Your willpower does not have to deplete every day if you have healthy habits already in place, a supreme confidence coupled with an unbreakable self-esteem, and an already strong willpower that's been strengthened and honed over time. Let's look at how you can achieve all of this to make yourself invincible to willpower depletion.

Developing Healthy Habits

When you start any self-improvement program, such as going on a new diet, your enthusiasm is already high and you're motivated by the pleasure of what you're trying to achieve or the pain of what you don't want to happen; however, your motivation will naturally diminish over time. When your motivation wanes, you'll rely on your willpower to get you through. Yet, no one has an endless supply, even if your willpower is virtually invincible. Every decision you have to make depletes that willpower slowly until you get to a point where it's gone or you've reached evening. The point of invincible willpower is to strengthen your willpower so much and avoid insignificant decisions throughout the day so that you don't run out by the evening.

Ninety-five percent of your life is dictated by your subconscious rather than your conscious decisions. This is the part of your brain that runs your life on autopilot. It's why you tie your shoes after you put them on, brush your teeth every morning, and drive a car without thinking about it. By consciously deciding to make a new habit, you're harnessing the power of your unconscious to make a new neural pathway in the brain. Once a new habit has become established, it's simple to do. Motivation and willpower are no longer necessary.

Therefore, to conserve willpower for those truly tough decisions, you need to turn your life into a series of habits or routine. It's important to start with only one habit because you'll easily get overwhelmed if you try to do more. Once you create one habit, you do something called habit stacking, which is where one habit is a trigger for another habit, such as brushing your teeth is a trigger for showering.

Here are the seven steps you can used to turn any desired activity into a habit. Once you've established the habit, you'll find you're doing it without thinking. These techniques can be used for current habits you want to change, and habits you want to create.

Step One: Set Small Goals

Setting a large goal, such as purchasing a new car, is exciting and fun, but starting with a small and boring goal is more likely to succeed. Small goals might be to meditate for ten minutes a day or to replace an unhealthy snack with raw vegetables. Another good one would be to walk for fifteen minutes per day. Taking a small action will trick your brain. Your subconscious prefers to be in control, and it hates change. Big changes will often upset the subconscious and it will become resistant, but you can sneak in small changes.

Step Two: Setup Triggers

Triggers are something that leads you to automatically do something else. For example, smokers are triggered to smoke after meals. Use these triggers to your advantage. If you make a commitment to meditate after lunch, then after a few weeks, you'll be meditating automatically after lunch. Visual triggers are good, too. Putting your workout clothes on the bed in the evening will encourage you to work out when you wake up in the morning.

Step Three: Do It Early

Meditating, exercising, or even transferring money into a savings account when your willpower is high in the morning will allow you to relax for the rest of the day. Make a healthy dinner ahead of time so you're not eating something unhealthy when you get home from work starving.

Step Four: Be Prepared

Be sure you have everything you need in order to be successful. If you want to begin a walking program, then get some comfortable shoes and a pedometer. If you want to start eating healthier, then throw away all the unhealthy snacks in your home and stock up on healthy ones.

Step Five: Make It Convenient

The more time-consuming and difficult it is to take an action, the less likely you'll be willing to do it. This is why so many people who purchase gym memberships drop out. Gyms just aren't that convenient to go to. Get everything you need ready ahead of time so that when it's time to get down to it, you can just do it.

Step Six: Make it Fun

If you don't like to do something, such as working out, then you're not going to stick with it. Find some way you can make your lifestyle change enjoyable, such as exercising with a friend, learning to cook healthy foods you enjoy, or finding a meditation program that speaks to you.

Step Seven: Don't Break Your Chain

Get yourself a calendar and hang it up somewhere you'll see it each day when you do your habit. When you do the habit, put an x on the calendar for that day. You don't want to see any blank days because this means you broke the chain. Use this for a month and you'll find you have a new habit formed already.

By using these seven steps to make a new habit or change an old one, you'll trick your brain into making a new neural pathway. Once that habit is formed, you can use it to serve as a beginning to bigger changes that will turn your life around.

Developing Supreme Confidence and Unbreakable Self-Esteem

Your confidence in your decisions and an unbreakable self-esteem are what make your willpower invincible. With supreme confidence, your decisions won't be overridden by what others are doing, and you'll be more likely to not need as much willpower to make a decision. If your self-esteem is healthy, then you won't need to second-guess everything you do. Confidence and self-esteem are imperative for success in life, but first, what are they?

What is Confidence?

There are two main things that contribute to your self-confidence, and these are your self-esteem and your self-efficacy. You obtain a sense of self-efficacy when you see yourself and others similar to you mastering skills and achieving their goals that matter in those skill areas. This is the confidence that if you were to learn and work hard in a certain area, then you'll succeed. It's the type of confidence that allows you to accept hard trials and persevere in the face of adversity.

This overlaps with self-esteem, which is the more general sense you're able to cope with what's happening in your life, and that you have a right to be happy. This comes from the feeling that the people around you approve of you, partly, which you might be able to or might not be able to control. However, it also comes from a sense that you're behaving morally or virtuously, that you're intelligent at what you do, and that you can compete successfully with others when you put your mind to it.

Some people believe self-confidence can be built up with positive thinking and affirmations. There is some truth in this, but it's just as important to build your self-confidence by setting and achieving your goals because this builds competence. Without competence as an underlying foundation, you don't have self-confidence. You have a shallow over-confidence with all the upset, issues, and failures that it brings.

Building Your Self-Confidence

Many people believe there's a quick fix for self-confidence through manipulating their minds, but the reality is, there isn't. The good news is more confidence is, readily achievable, as long as you have the focus and the determination to get to the end result of more confidence. The things you'll do to build your self-confidence are going to build your success.

So without further ado, here are the steps to building your self-confidence.

Step One: Prepare Yourself

The first step involves getting ready for the journey to self-confidence. You have to take an inventory of where you are in life, think about where you'd like to go, and get yourself in the proper mindset for the journey. Commit yourself to beginning the journey and sticking with it. Here are the five things you need to do in order to prepare for the journey.

1. Look at what you've already attained. Think about your life from the start to the present,

and list the ten best things you accomplished in an Accomplishment Journal. Maybe you were the quarterback for your high school football team, you scored the highest on the SAT scores in your state, you aced an exam you studied hard for, you graduated college, or maybe you obtained a really amazing job. Put these in a document where you can look at them often, and then spend a few minutes every week enjoying the successes you've already accomplished.

2. Think about your strengths. While looking at your Accomplishment Journal, reflecting on your past achievements, think about what your friends would consider your strengths and weaknesses. From these, think about the threats and the opportunities you face. Make sure you enjoy a few minutes to reflect on your strengths.

3. Think about what's important to you and where you'd like to be in the future. Setting and attaining your goals is a key part of this step, and real confidence is going to come from this. Goal setting is the process you use to set up target for yourself and measure your

success at hitting those targets. You'll learn more about goal setting in the final chapter of this book. Set goals that will exploit your strengths, minimize weaknesses, control the threats you face, and realize your opportunities.

4. Start managing your thoughts. Learn to pick up on and defeat your negative self-talk, which will destroy your confidence. Remember the internal willpower killer of limiting beliefs and the section about common limiting belief statements? Recognize when you're having a thought like one of those statements and turn it around into a positive statement.

5. Commit yourself to success. The final part of preparing for your journey is to make a clear and concise promise to yourself that you'll be completely committed to this journey, and that you will do everything you have to in order to achieve it. If you find you're having doubts surface as you do this final step, write them down and challenge them rationally and calmly. If they dissolve when you scrutinize them, that's excellent. However, if they're

based in reality and on genuine risks, be sure you set additional goals to manage these doubts correctly.

Your self-confidence is about balance. At one of the spectrum, there are people who have a low self-confidence, and at the other end are those who are over-confident. You want to be in the middle with a healthy confidence.

If you're under-confident, you'll avoid risks and avoid stretching yourself to your potential, and you might not try in the first place. If you're over-confident, you'll take on one too many risks and stretch yourself beyond your capabilities, and then you'll crash. You might find you're so optimistic that you don't try your best in order to succeed.

Step Two: Set Out

This is where you're going to begin slowly, moving toward your goal at a steady pace. By doing the right things and beginning with easy wins, you'll be on the path to success, and you'll begin building self-confidence.

There are four easy steps to this step.

1. Obtain the knowledge necessary to succeed. Identify the skills you'll need to achieve your goals, and then look at what it will take to obtain these skills. Don't accept a just-good-enough solution. Look for the right solution, a course or program that will fully train you and educate you to achieve what you'd like to attain, and gives you a qualification or a certificate you can be proud of.

2. Focus on the basics. When you begin, don't try to do something elaborate or clever. Don't reach for perfection, either. Just enjoy doing easy things well.

3. Set small goals and then complete them. Begin with small goals you identified in step one, and get in the habit of setting new ones. Get into the habit of completing them and celebrating your achievements. Little by little, you'll pile on the successes.

4. Manage your mind. Make sure you stay on top of thinking positively, celebrating, and enjoying your successes, as well as keeping those mental images strong. Learn to handle failure at the same time. Accept that mistakes are going to happen when you're trying to do

something new. In fact, if you get in the habit of treating your mistakes as a learning experience instead, you will begin to see them positively.

Step Three: Move toward Success

At this point, you'll feel your confidence building. Some of the courses you started in step two will be finished and you'll have successes to celebrate. This is the time to begin stretching yourself beyond your perceived limits. Make your goals a little bigger and your challenges a little tougher. Increase the sizes of your commitments, and extend those skills you learned into new arenas.

Make sure you keep yourself grounded at the same time. This is where you might get a little over-confident and stretch yourself too thin.

As long as you keep stretching yourself enough, but not too far, you'll find your confidence building. You'll have earned your self-confidence because you put in the hard time and effort necessary to do so. Goal setting is one of the most important skills you can learn to improve your self-confidence. We'll discuss that more in chapter six.

For right now, let's move on to your self-esteem.

What is Self-Esteem?

Your self-esteem is just as imperative as your self-confidence. Your self-esteem is how you value yourself. It's how you perceive your value to the world and how valuable you believe you are to those around you. Self-esteem will affect your trust in others, your relationships, your work, and almost every other part of your life. Positive self-esteem will give you the flexibility and strength to take charge of your life and grow from your mistakes without fearing failure or rejection. Having a high self-esteem will ensure you do not run out of willpower because you're constantly making decisions to please others. You'll be making the right decisions for yourself.

Some signs of a high self-esteem include:

- Self-direction
- Confidence
- An awareness of your personal strengths and weaknesses
- The capability to make mistakes and learn from them

- The ability to come up with solutions to solve problems
- Optimism
- Independence
- Feeling comfortable with your emotions
- The ability to trust others
- A good sense of your personal limitations
- The capability to say no

Some signs of a low self-esteem include:

- A negative viewpoint on life
- Perfectionism
- Mistrusting those around you, even those who are showing you signs of affection
- Blaming others
- Fear of taking any risks
- Feelings of being unlovable and unloved
- Letting others make decisions for you
- Fear of being ridiculed

Building Your Self-Esteem

There are six steps to building your self-esteem, which will build your self-confidence and willpower in return. These steps may not be easy in the beginning, but they're well worth the effort.

Step One: Take an Inventory of Your Self-Esteem

You can't fix what you're not aware of. Before you begin working on putting cognitive-behavioral therapy to work, you need to spend a lot of time identifying your irrational thoughts and behaviors. The same is true for self-esteem.

If you generalize and say, "I'm not a good person and I suck at my job. I can't do anything right," then you're telling yourself a simple and convincing lie. Those words aren't true. Everyone sucks from time to time. Wallowing in it isn't the solution, but acknowledging it and moving on is.

So here's what you need to do. Get a piece of paper and put a line down the middle or fold it in half to make a line. On the right hand side, you should write down 'Strengths' at the top, and on the left-hand side, you should write 'Weaknesses.' Now, list ten on either side of the line. That might seem like a lot of strengths if you're suffering from a low self-esteem, but you'll find ten if you look hard enough.

If you have a lot of difficulty coming up with all ten, think about what others told you about yourself over the years. Maybe it was praise from a friend or family member for when you listened to them when they had a problem, or your boss told you that you did a really great job at work on a project. Someone may have told you that you were good at cleaning, telling stories, writing, singing, or dancing. No matter what the strength is, or how silly it might seem, write it down anyway. You'll be surprised by how easy it is to come up with all ten when you approach it from this direction.

Congratulations; you've come up with your Self-Esteem Inventory! This will tell you all the things you already tell yourself about your weaknesses, as well as show you that there are just as many good things to say about yourself. Some of the weaknesses you might be able to change, if you work on them one at a time, and it might take you a lot of time to fix them. Remember, no one changes overnight, so don't setup unrealistic goals or expectations that you can change things in just a week, which brings us to the next step.

Step Two: Set Realistic Expectations

Nothing kills your self-esteem more than setting up unrealistic expectations for yourself or others. As an example, people who are in their twenties see themselves as being millionaires with homes and fancy cars by the time they're in their thirties, and by the time they get to thirty, they don't get there. They believe they're failures because of it. By the time you hit thirty, if you're still in your twenties, you'll most likely be in more debt than ever and you won't be close to being a millionaire, and your self-esteem will take a huge blow.

Sometimes expectations can be smaller but they're still unrealistic. For example, "I wish my parents would stop criticizing me." Most likely, your parents never will stop criticizing you, but that's no reason to allow their criticism to affect your view of yourself, or your self-worth. Check your expectations if they continue to disappoint you. Your self-esteem is certainly going to thank you.

Checking your expectations can help you stop the cycle of negative thinking about yourself that reinforces your negative self-esteem. When you set realistic expectations, you can stop beating yourself up for not meeting an idealistic goal.

Step Three: Set Aside Perfectionism and Embrace Accomplishments and Mistakes

Perfectionism is not something that will happen for anyone, so you need to let the idea of it go. You're never going to be perfect; you won't have a perfect body, a perfect life, a perfect child, a perfect relationship, or a perfect home. Everyone revels in the idea of perfection because they see so much of it on television, in magazines, or in the movies, but that's just an artificial creation of society. Perfectionism doesn't exist.

Instead of aiming for perfectionism, celebrate your achievements as you achieve them. Acknowledge them to yourself for their true value. Don't devalue what you do because you perceive it to be easy. It might help to keep a journal or a list of the things you accomplish in life. Some people might do this on a daily basis, while others might feel comfortable noting achievements once a week or once a month. The key is to get to the smaller goals and move on from each of them.

It's just as imperative that you take something away from the mistakes you've made and will make in life. It doesn't mean you're worthless or a bad person if you make mistakes. It just means you've made a mistake like everyone else on this planet. Welcome to the human race. Mistakes are an opportunity for growth and learning. If you push yourself out of the negative self-talk or the self-pity you're wallowing in after a mistake, we'll be able to learn from it.

Step Four: Explore Who You Are

Some of the most well-adjusted people you will ever meet have gone through this exercise of exploring themselves. It's not about just knowing your strengths and weaknesses, but about opening yourself up to opportunities as they come, trying something new, opening yourself up to new thoughts, new viewpoints, and friendships.

Sometimes when your self-esteem has taken a huge hit and you're feeling down, you might feel like you have nothing to offer others or the world. It might be that you just haven't found everything you do have to offer, such as things you haven't even considered or even thought of yet. Learning what they are is a matter of trial and error. It's how you become the person you've always dreamed of being, by taking risks and trying new things that you wouldn't ordinarily try.

Step Five: Be Open to Adjusting Your Self-Image

Self-esteem is not useful if it's based on an older version of who you were that doesn't exist anymore. Everyone used to be good at a lot of things that they're just not good at anymore. Some people may have excelled in calculus, but they couldn't do a math problem today to save their lives. Some people used to be able to play an instrument and no longer can. There are skills we've had that we lose over time because we don't practice them all the time.

But that's alright. Adjust your beliefs about yourself and your strengths as you go along in life. You can become better at something else, such as being a better writer, being a better editor, or being a better guitar player. Stop sitting around and wishing you could do things like you used to. If you continue to think about it so much that is bothers you, maybe it's time to pick up the skill again, but otherwise, let it go and evaluate yourself on what's happening in your life right now.

Make sure you adjust your self-image and your self-esteem to match your current skills and capabilities, not those you harbored in the past.

Step Six: Stop Comparing Yourself to Others

There's nothing worse that can hurt your self-esteem more than an unfair comparison. Let's say your best friend has 1,500 Facebook friends while you only have 100 Facebook friends. Maybe your brother or sister is better at finances than you are, or perhaps your coworker outperformed you at work. Perhaps your neighbor's house is a bit bigger than yours. You can see how these things might impact your feelings about yourself, the more you do this type of thing.

It's difficult, but you have to stop comparing yourself to those around you. The only person you need to be comparing yourself to is yourself. These comparisons aren't fair because you don't know as much as you believe you do about those people's lives, or what it's actually like to be them. You believe it's better, but their lives could be a lot worse than you imagine, and in most cases, they are. For example, maybe your best friend paid for all those friends, or perhaps your brother or sister is better at finances because they're stealing from work.

Once you complete all of these steps, you will be able to strengthen your self-esteem and see yourself for what you're really worth, which is a lot more than you believe now. It may take some time to work on this, and it's not as easy as using affirmations or faux positive thinking, but it'll be worth it in the end. It takes effort in order to accomplishment something, so stick with it.

Simple Exercises to Develop Willpower and Strengthen It

You now know how to improve your self-esteem and your self-confidence, but what about improving your willpower in the meantime? Your willpower cannot be invincible without a little bit of exercise, but how do you do that? Take a look at these simple exercises to help you strengthen and develop your willpower.

Meditate for 10 Minutes

Meditation is one of the quickest and easiest ways to exercise your willpower. When you meditate, you train your brain to focus and resist the urge to think about something else. Researchers have discovered that meditating for just two to three days for ten minutes allows you brain to focus better, energizes you, and reduces your stress levels, and we all need stress reduction!

To get started with ten minutes of meditation, try practicing the deep breathing exercises from chapter four.

Improve Your Posture

Remember the study where students were asked to work on their posture for two weeks? Every time they found themselves slouching, they were instructed to correct themselves by sitting up straight (Muraven, Longitudinal improvement of self-regulation through practice: building self-control strength through repeated exercise, 1999). This practice improves their perseverance on other willpower tests.

To get started, just correct your posture every time you find yourself slouching while you're working and while you're at home. It sounds very simple, but it actually takes willpower to sit up straight. Every time you do this, you're doing one rep of your willpower muscles.

Keep a Food Diary

The same study discovered that those who kept a food diary were able to improve their willpower. Most people don't log all the food they eat during the day, so it will take willpower to keep track of it all. Any similar recording of information works too, but a food diary is a good one because it tells you a lot about your eating habits, and whether they're healthy or not.

To get started, you can download an app or you can just keep a list on your phone or computer. Keep a diary for two weeks of what you eat, and you'll increase your resistance to eating unhealthy foods.

Use Your Non-Dominant Hand

This is the same methodology as the posture exercise. Researchers conducted studies testing other corrective actions, and one that worked especially well was to use your non-dominant hand. So if you're right handed, use your left hand. Your brain's wired to use the dominant hand, so it will take willpower to use your opposite hand.

To start this exercise, carve out a hunk of your day where you will use your opposite hand. It doesn't have to be for more than an hour to obtain results. If you aim for more than an hour, you could tire out your willpower muscles unnecessarily, so don't do it for too long.

Correct Your Words

Another study conducted by researchers was to change a subject's natural speech. This included resisting the urge to use swear words, or saying 'hello' rather than saying 'hey.' Again, it took willpower to consciously go against their instincts. How you correct your speech doesn't matter, as long as you're changing your natural speech habits and patterns (Baumeister, Gailliot, & DeWall, 2006).

To get started, carve out a time during the day when you will practice and choose the words you'll change. You could try not using swear words, try not using contractions, or try to use a proper sentence structure for every thought for an hour a day. Do this for just two weeks and you'll improve your willpower greatly.

Make Self-Imposed Deadlines and Meet Them

If you ever attended grade school or college, you remember what it was like cramming for a test or doing last minute papers. Your willpower is taxed as you try to tune out distractions and you become hyper-productive. Using this same idea, researchers discovered that by making self-imposed deadlines, you can work your willpower in the same way.

To get started, just pick a task on your to-do list that you might have put off. Set a deadline for accomplishing that task, and be sure you adhere to the deadline. If you follow this for two weeks, you'll not only get your old to-do's finished, but you'll improve your overall life by exercising more, improving your diet, and cutting back on drugs and alcohol. It seems that by improving one area of your life, you improve all the others too. (Baumeister, Gailliot, & DeWall, 2006).

Track Your Spending

In the same way most people don't track the food they eat, many people don't track how much they spend either. Even if you're not cutting back on spending, which would be a willpower workout, researchers discovered that just keeping track of where you're spending your money improves your willpower (Oaten & Cheng, 2007).

To get started with this, try a budget application you can use on your phone or your computer. You can connect it to your bank account, credit card, and any other type of account to keep track of your purchases automatically. By just reviewing this daily, you'll increase your focus and capability to resist unrelated temptations, such as unhealthy snacks.

Squeeze a Handgrip

For those who are truly determined and want to increase their willpower greatly, squeeze a handgrip until your hand is exhausted. If you've ever squeezed one of these before, you know it will give you a forearm burn. It takes willpower to keep squeezing one of these.

To get started, purchase a handgrip and squeeze it with each hand until you feel exhausted. Willing yourself to squeeze even after it's exhausting increases your willpower on other tasks.

Carry Something Tempting Around

For those who are really determined and need something a little more difficult, you could increase your capability to say 'no' by carrying around something you want but can't have all day. For example, if you enjoy sweets, then carry around a piece of candy in your pocket all day. If you're able to resist it, you're much more likely to resist other temptations, too.

To get started, learn how to resist cravings. This is going to be hard, so you'll want to know how to deal with them. Then, carry something around that's small but tempting in your pocket. It doesn't have to be for the whole day, but for long enough that you'll feel temptation. By saying 'no' to yourself consistently, you'll increase your willpower.

Be Aware of Your Automatic Decisions

One final exercise is to be mindful of your decisions as you go about your day. People are often so lost in their thoughts that their actions just fall into place. Taking the time to think about why you're making your decisions on a daily basis increases your ability to focus and resist temptations.

To try this out, catch yourself in an automatic behavior and ask yourself why you're doing that behavior. This might be questioning why you're eating an egg rather than cereal for breakfast, or why you're putting sugar in your coffee. Any way you can think consciously about an automatic behavior increases your self-control and willpower.

In the final chapter, we're going to talk about how to use your invincible willpower to grab hold of life and accomplish the goals you've always dreamed of accomplishing.

Chapter Six – Using Your Willpower to Accomplish Your Goals

Without willpower, accomplishing goals is impossible. You have to exercise a certain amount of willpower in order to achieve something, but if you have invincible willpower and are able to stick with the necessary steps to accomplishing a goal, you will achieve it much sooner. That means you can move on to accomplishing another goal quicker, which means you end up accomplishing a lot more in your life than you would have if you lacked willpower.

In this first section, we're going to discuss what a reasonable goal is by outlining the SMART goal system. It's one of the most common systems used because it truly works.

SMART Goals

SMART stands for Specific, Measurable, Attainable, Realistic, and Timely.

Specific

Specific goals have a much better chance of being attained rather than a general goal. There are six questions you need to answer in order to setup a specific goal.

1. Who's involved?
2. What do you want to achieve?
3. Where will you achieve it?
4. When will you achieve it?
5. What are the requirements and constraints of the goal?
6. Why do you want to accomplish this goal?

As an example, you would not want to have a goal of getting in shape. A specific goal would be something such as, "Join a gym and workout for three days per week for half an hour."

Measurable

Create concrete criteria for measuring the progress toward the achievement of the goals you set. Measuring your progress helps you stay on track, keep up with your target deadlines, and experience the joy of achievement that keeps you going on the your current path to reaching your end goal. To figure out if your goal is measurable, ask yourself the following questions.

1. How much or how many?
2. How will you know when the goal is completed?

Attainable

When you identify a goal that's important to you, you start to figure out methods you can use to make those goals come true. You attain the abilities, attitudes, financial capacity, and skills to obtain your goals. You start to see previously overlooked opportunities that will bring you closer to the attainment of your goals.

You can attain just about any goal you set up when you plan steps wisely and create a timeframe that lets you complete those steps. Goals that might have appeared to be unattainable and out of reach will get closer and grow into being more achievable, not because your goals have minimized, but because you grew and expanded to match those goals. When you list goals, you build self-image. You see yourself as being worthy of those goals, and develop the personality and traits that will let you complete them.

Realistic

In order for a goal to be realistic, a goal has to represent and objective that you are both willing and able to work toward. A goal is able to be both realistic and high. You are the only person who is able to decide how high your goal ought to be, but you should be sure that each goal signifies considerable progress.

High goals are frequently easier to reach than low goals because low goals exert low motivational force. Some of the hardest things you've ever accomplished will seem easy because they were a labor of love and passion.

Your goal is realistic if you believe it's attainable. Other ways you can know if your goal is realistic is to figure out if you've accomplished something similar in the past or you've asked yourself what conditions need to exist in order to accomplish the goal.

Timely

Make sure your goals are within timeframes. With no timeframe tied to the goal, there is no sense of urgency. If you want to lose fifty pounds, when do you want to lose them by? Someday is not a good enough answer, but if you anchor that goal with a timeframe, such as by January 1st, then you'll setup your subconscious mind to achieve that goal and start working on it.

Tips for Harnessing Your Willpower to Achieve Goals

You understand how to create SMART goals, but how do you harness your willpower in order to achieve those goals?

Here are a few tips and techniques you can use to build up your self-control and attain your goals.

1. Focus on only one goal at a time. Psychologists have discovered it's more effective for someone to focus on a single, clear goal or task rather than taking on a list of many goals at one time. Succeeding at your first goal frees up your willpower so that you can be devoted to your next goal. Work on one behavior at a time, such as meditating for ten minutes in the morning or setting aside twenty minutes a day to workout.

2. Avoid temptations in order to conserve on willpower. Avoiding temptations is a good tactic for maintaining your self-control. Keeping temptations out of the house is

helpful, but if you can't do that, then at least keep them out of sight. This approach works excellently for many scenarios. It's important to have a work area that's conducive to getting work done with very few distractions. When you need to focus, turn off your phone, sign out of your email, and get rid of any other distractions. That's an example of removing temptation and avoiding it.

3. Have a plan ready. Having a plan in place can help you fight enticements without having to use your willpower. Figure out how you will react to a situation ahead of time and you'll have more resolve.

4. Monitor your behavior toward your end goal. Create a reasonable plan to meet your end goal and recommit every day to making progress toward that goal. If you want to save more money, then transfer five dollars to your savings account every day. Research has shown that recording your behavior makes you more aware and

helps you change that behavior, so doing something on a daily basis allows you to stay on track.

5. Reward yourself. When you reach a milestone in your goal, reward yourself for doing a good job, but make sure the reward isn't conflicting with the changes you're trying to make. Don't eat a bowl of ice cream when you lose ten pounds. Don't spend fifteen dollars when you just saved money. Instead, take some time to engage in something you enjoy but is still healthy and conducive to your goal. For example, if you're working on tight deadlines, get up and move around every now and again to reward yourself with a small break.

6. Get enough sleep. Sleep deprivation will affect your willpower and how your body and mind uses energy. This will affect how well you can resist temptations. When you don't get enough sleep, your willpower is more likely to fail. However, just one

night of good sleep helps boost your self-control.

7. Find support. Having a support system will help you reach your goals. Surround yourself with individuals you trust and know are going to be understanding of your goals. They should be willing to help you succeed.

Once you achieve a single goal, your willpower will increase substantially. You'll be able to see that you can achieve anything you set your mind to, and this means you can set more substantial goals in the future.

Conclusion

When you put it all together, it seems like it's a lot to take in and a lot to work on, but your first goal should be working on your internal influences. Once you've come to grips with who you are and you understand that your negative self-talk, limiting beliefs, and lack of self-control are not helping you, then you can move forward by battling those influences. The next step is to take a look at your outside world. What is keeping you from achieving your goals around you? Are your friends not very supportive? Do you spend too much time worrying about your finances when you could automate them? Fix your exterior influences and limit them to the positive ones.

The next step is to create your invincible willpower by working on developing healthy habits, a supreme confidence and unbreakable self-esteem, and strengthening your willpower with exercises. All of these will have small goals or steps throughout the process that will lead up to one ultimate goal, which is achieving an invincible willpower you can use to attain your dreams.

While it might seem like a lot, it's well worth it in the end. Your life will be improved greatly, and you'll be proud to be who you are. I hope you're able to attain an invincible willpower after you work on the goals within this book.

If you enjoyed what you read and found it useful, then please leave a review at your online Book retailer's website.

Thank you for reading!

References

Ashraf, N., Karlan, D. S., & Yin, W. (2004,
December 9). *SEED: A Commitment
Savings Product in the Philippines.*
Retrieved from seedpolicy.pdf:
https://ashrafnava.files.wordpress.com/2
016/07/seedpolicy.pdf

Baumeister, R. F., Gailliot, M., & DeWall, N. C.
(2006). Self-Regulation and Personality:
How Interventions Increase Regulatory
Success, and How Depletion Moderates
the Effects of Traits on Behavior. *Journal
of Personality*, 1774-1797.

Christakis, N. A., & James, F. H. (2007). The
Spread of Obesity in a Large Social
Network over 32 Years. *The New England
Journal of Medicine*, 370-379.

Duckworth, A. L., & Seligman, M. E. (2005).
*Self-Discipline Outdoes IQ in Predicting
Academic Performance of Adolescents.*
Retrieved from Psychological Science:

http://www.sas.upenn.edu/~duckwort/images/PsychologicalScienceDec2005.pdf

Inzlicht, M., & Schmeichel, B. J. (2012). What Is Ego Depletion? Toward a Mechanistic Revision of the Resource Model of Self-Control. *Perspectives on Psychological Science*, 450-463.

Mischel, W. (1989). Delay of gratification in children. *Science*, 933-938.

Moffitt, T. E., Arseneault, L., Belsky, D., Dickson, N., Hancox, R. J., Harrington, H., . . . Caspi, A. (2011). A gradient of childhood self-control predicts health, wealth, and public safety. *CrossMark*, 2693-2698.

Muraven, M. (1999). Longitudinal improvement of self-regulation through practice: building self-control strength through repeated exercise. *Journal of Social Psychology*, 446-457.

Muraven, M. (2010). Practicing self-control lowers the risk of smoking lapse. *Psychology of Addictive Behaviors*, 446-452.

Oaten, M., & Cheng, K. (2007). Improvements in self-control from financial monitoring. *Journal of Economic Psychology*, 487-501.

Vohs, K. D., Baumeister, R. F., & Schmeichel, B. J. (2012). Motivation, personal beleifs, and limited resources all contribute to self-control. *Journal of Experimental Social Psychology*, 943-947.

Vohs, K., & Faber, R. (2003). Self-Regulation and Impulsive Spending Patterns. *Advances in Consumer Research*, 125-126.

38966718R00061

Made in the USA
Middletown, DE
01 January 2017